NUMB3R3D W8RDS

BERWICK AUGUSTIN

EVOKE180 PUBLISHING | LAUDERHILL, FL

NUMBERED WORDS
Copyright © 2017 by Berwick Augustin
Published by Evoke180
Lauderhill, FL
www.evoke180.com

All rights reserved. Except as permitted under the U.S. Copyright Act of 1976, no part of this publication may be reproduced, distributed, stored in a retrieval system, or transmitted in any form or by any means-electronic, mechanical, digital, photocopy, recording, or any other-except for brief quotations in printed reviews, without the prior written permission of the publisher.

ISBN 978-0-9991822-0-8

Printed in the United States of America

BERWICK AUGUSTIN

Berwick Augustin is a writer and educator whose work can be described as a sponge that has been soaked with a strong blend of culture and spirituality. He is the founder of Evoke180 LLC, a literary movement that uses poetry and theater to fuse the arts and multiculturalism into well-blended body of works to edify the international community.

Berwick Augustin is available for lectures, readings, live performances, writing workshops, and educational consulting. For more information regarding his availability, please visit berwickaugustin.com.

DEDICATION

To my beautiful wife, Gretchen Augustin,
for supporting my artistic endeavors
and her godly devotion to
mothering our three children.

TABLE OF CONTENTS

1. 1
2. 2
3. 3
4. 4
5. 5
6. 6
7. 7
8. 8
9. 9
10. 10
11. 11
12. 12
13. 13
14. 14
15. 15
16. 16
17. 17
18. 18
19. 19
20. 20
21. 21
22. 22
23. 23
24. 24

25.	25
26.	26
27.	27
28.	28
29.	29
30.	30
31.	31
32.	32
33.	33
34.	34
35.	35
36.	36
37.	37
38.	38
39.	39
40.	40
41.	41
42.	42
43.	43
44.	44
45.	45
46.	46
47.	47
48.	48
49.	49
50.	50

NUMBERED WORDS

1.

Transfiguration.

2.

Speaking
Feelings.

NUMBERED WORDS

3.

Words
Action
Revolution.

4.

Confess
All
Wrongdoings.
Forgiveness.

NUMBERED WORDS

5.

Love is
always
at war.

6.

Temptation comes to all! Self-control.

NUMBERED WORDS

7.

Always
love
when hated.
Pray
when persecuted.

8.

Revenge
sweeter when
earthly laws
can't summon avenger.

NUMBERED WORDS

9.

Choices
are crucial,
choose wisely
life
depends on them.

10.

Patience
is married to faith.
Doubt
can cause a divorce.

11.

Gratitude
is watching the world
through
the bifocal lens of optimism.

12.

Hearts
harden
intimacy is an inmate
to isolation
love
begins
to
fade…

13.

Regret
is a neighbor
you keep inviting over
but
don't really want around.

14.

Love
is
genuine.
It
goes hard,
soothe smoothly,
constantly resets
to refresh
its commitment.

15.

Fail better!
Forget disappointments quickly.
If you miscarry an opportunity,
labor on the next one.

16.

The desire
to do what's right
can be defeated
by the ability to carry it out.

17.

Leadership
compassion, courage, consistent
faith, failure, fortitude
heavy, hard, humility
patience, persistence, prayer
selfless, strong, servant
Lead.

18.

Commitment
Words draw the message
the lips do the honor of delivery,
but the heart produces the reverence.

19.

State of the human address
hearts defiled by wickedness
murder, slander, pride, foolishness
the answer is Jesus and righteousness.

20.

The discipline to win
demands battle of the mind.
Train the brain
to shift perspective
beyond present circumstances.
Foresee victory.

21.

Well of words is dry.
Difficult to write
through writer's block.
Words on a cliff,
but refuse to fall on paper.

22.

REgrets
Instant REplays of unwise actions.
Brain ceaselessly REferees emotions
REminds the mind
to REwind THAT time…
Trigger REactions
unforgiveness RElapses
Again.

23.

Faith
Reckless at best
detrimental when dormant
hope desperately depends on it
sight is independent of it
believe before you see
blind trust.

24.

Grace
undeserved kindness
unmerited favor
flavor unsweetened by reproach
envied cavity
unexpected arrival
tickled blessings
goose bumps bumping differences
into the abyss of forgiveness.

25.

Reconcile
Picking up the pieces
broken relationships
Trusting the power of forgiveness
To glue happy memories together
eradicate rotten recollections
Plant mustard seed of faith.

26.

Justice
please roll like a river
through inner city streets
like never failing righteousness
falling from heaven.
Cops
play God
take lives
stir wrath
Love mourns.

27.

Memory
Name evaporates
Legacy lingers
Memory perpetuates
Generations remember
Remembrance mistreated
Tainted tribute
Spoiled praise
Esteemed existence
Heralded homage
Revered respect
Admired accolades
Discipled duties
Ever-present presence

28.

Unity
creates
power
when used as a rope
that binds virtues together.
Maintained unison gives birth to hope
unbreakable peace
harmony reigns, division cease
The gospel is released.

29.

Peace
is a delicious pie
envied by all.
A
piece
of
peace
is packed with flavors
that slice through cerebral palettes.
Piece
of savoring harmony is
peace
of mind.

30.

Technology
antisocial on social media
Hypocritical advancement
Blind to bird's eye view
tweet
hash tag
like
post
Instagram
blog
Share Jesus' status:
'forsake all followers and family to follow me.'

31.

Potential
If given a chance
potential would:
give chance all it can handle,
dismantle disadvantages and disproportions,
high beams on the eyes of the heart,
enlighten inherited hope within.
Greatness awakens.

32.

Exhausted mind
labored thoughts
reflections wailing in wilderness
tears plunging in the forest of regrets
insomnia is insane
rest is restless
God designs resilience into relationships
To save broken hearts and minds.

33.

Forgiveness is not reconciliation
releasing the pain and the person
from prison in your brain
isn't automatic access
to the reconciliation process.
Heart engaged in renewed relationship
is intentional practice with a purpose.

34.

They can't break you!
They don't know what you've been through.
Your life is seasoned with storms
all you see is rough seas
satan suffers hypertension
every time you sprinkle salt on the earth.

35.

Leaders
Simple servant
complex responsibility.
Character
on the front line,
vulnerable to attacks
Essential to victory.
Position
comes with power
purpose is to inspire
duty is heavy
weight unsurmountable
the changes
leaders
evoke
linger forever.

36.

Hopelessness
sharing hope with the hopeless
is like
a drowning voice in a sea of despair.
Keep praying
when there seems to be no answer
Remember
God's goodness is not tied
to the rightness of circumstances.

37.

Restoration
it's difficult to undo what has been done.
Reconnect, restore, move on
is easier said than done.
What would cause love to leave
the scene of a crime
filled with murderous emotions
and a dying heart?

38.

Tamed Courage
strength to stand
in the midst of pain
and difficulties isn't easily attained.
The rage in cou-rage
has to be balanced before
Success takes the stage.
Fear dissipates
nervousness is put to sleep
uncomfortable becomes normal.

39.

Broken heart
is so difficult to spell
dispel phonics and internalize
the learned lessons written
on each fragmented part
before God reshapes the pieces
into a stronger heart
purposed
to help someone else
in the future.
Never waste hurt!

40.

Make way for Yahweh
Undisputed champion
Solely cultivates *Holy fields.*
Losing lost its sting
I'm in this ring
against life
with a gospel right quicker than *Ali,*
more ferocious than *Tyson*
winning every bout God *May- weather* storm my way.

41.

No one's born an expert.
Learning only comes through failure
the closer you get to the cross,
the lower your selfish coffin
inches six feet underground.
Scribble these syllables on my tombstone
"he lives, it's Christ; he dies, it's gain."

42.

Festered
Life threatening feelings
undealt pain
gangrene anger
sitting on the heart's chamber
feasting on resentment's mildew
Who knew something brand new
would become so rotten.
Godless intentions, Christ-less actions
lead to hellish tears
Fester or forgive
The latter is heaven mandated.

43.

Truth
Truth has no twins!
It stands alone
on veracity mountain
Shining on carbon copies.
Second place finisher
First loser to genuine authority.
As an original,
live life the way the originator
originated your origin
Christ is the way, the truth, the life.

44.

One way
Believe, love, obey
Anything otherwise
is a deadly invitation,
head on collision
With ruin, ritual, religion,
Asinine coasting through the motion.
Christ-like commitment
is an exclusive one way road
that leads to golden streets.
Unbiblical moral
is a broad way to destruction.

45.

God's 45
Caliber higher than any conceived power
Fire powder releases through the gospel
Christ is the ammo
expands through scripture
engrained in the heart's chamber
locks in the brain
fires through actions
unlocks ungodliness
extracts disobedience
ejects pride
cocks Christlikeness
pulls trigger
undying love.

46.

I wanna paralyze you
with my love
so I can fix you up again!
Gracious honor to have broken
the seal of your secret garden
making love under
the mistletoe of romance
soothes my soul.
Thank God for the experience
of ecstasy through marriage
with you.

47.

Distractions
Destroy precious time.
Wasted
Yesterday is not recyclable.
Irreversible
Tomorrow has yet to be attained.
Uncontrollable
Today is my best weapon.
Inconceivable
Opportunities evaporated.
Unimaginable
Destiny is finger tips away,
but slide through slippery fingers.
Unthinkable
Friend turned to foe,
foe camouflaged as friend
Smokescreen diversions.

48.

Choices
Stuck
at a fork on the road
desire shifting between turn signals
right..
left…
brain parked on confusion
starving to understand
which turn
is cosigned by wisdom.
Decision feasting on the mind
time gluttonous partner in crime
road to peace of mind
is a standstill land mine.

49.

Servants
sent to serve
never seek to be served.
Entrusted to shepherd sheeps
flocking for love along pastures
like a pastor.
Practice patience impregnated by humility
sacrifice self as ransom for many
hands-on personality
harvest is plenty
workers are few
solitary loneliness
rewards are beyond the labor
Selfless ambassadors.

50.

Infinite spirit, spoken word
word of life, word made flesh
proclaimed king, peasant lifestyle
betrayed, rejected, homeless
alienated, oppressed, afflicted
Forgiving
willingly gave up His life
hung on a cross
reverse the curse
of future generations
unmerited favor
undeserved grace
death chauffeured
in salvation's hurst
there's no us without Jesus.

www.ingramcontent.com/pod-product-compliance
Lightning Source LLC
Chambersburg PA
CBHW070441010526
44118CB00014B/2137